Meeting Challenges

Program Authors

Connie Juel, Ph.D.

Jeanne R. Paratore, Ed.D.

Deborah Simmons, Ph.D.

Sharon Vaughn, Ph.D.

Glenview, Illinois
Boston, Massachusetts
Chandler, Arizona
Upper Saddle River, New Jersey

ISBN-13: 978-0-328-45292-7
ISBN-10:   0-328-45292-0

7 8 9 10 V011 14 13
CC1

Meeting Challenges

Courage 5

Why do people act courageously?

Natural Disasters 31

How can nature challenge us?

Contents

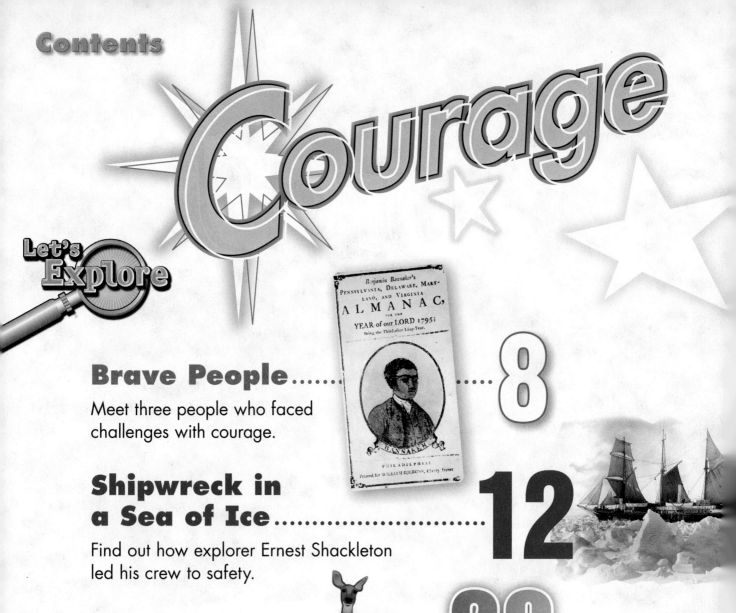

Courage

Let's Explore

Words 2 the Wise

There are many different ways to show **courage.** As you read, think about what it means to be brave.

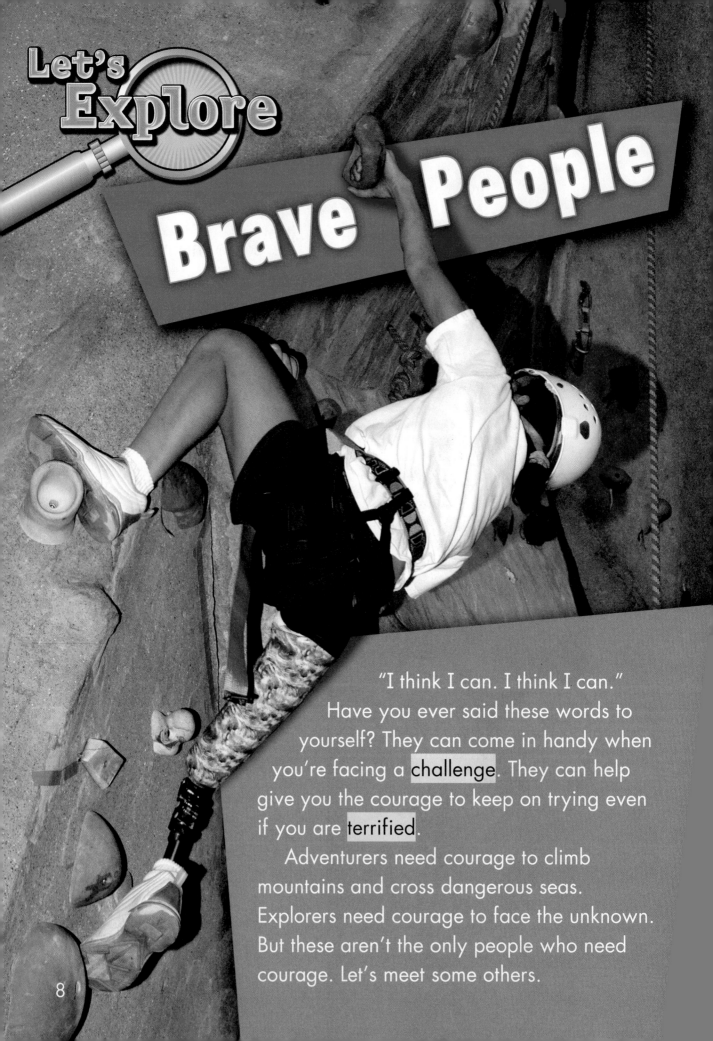

Let's Explore

Brave People

"I think I can. I think I can."
Have you ever said these words to
yourself? They can come in handy when
you're facing a challenge. They can help
give you the courage to keep on trying even
if you are terrified.

Adventurers need courage to climb
mountains and cross dangerous seas.
Explorers need courage to face the unknown.
But these aren't the only people who need
courage. Let's meet some others.

Benjamin Banneker needed courage to prove people wrong. In the 1700s, many people thought African Americans could not achieve great things. Banneker, who was African American, studied science and math. He also observed the night sky. He learned to predict how the stars and planets move. Using this knowledge, he wrote an almanac.* His skill impressed many people.

Banneker also wrote to Thomas Jefferson. He challenged Jefferson to work hard to end false ideas about African Americans. In turn, Jefferson praised Banneker's knowledge and effort. Banneker's bravery helped change people's attitudes toward African Americans.

***almanac** yearly booklet of facts about weather, tides, and the rising times of the sun and moon

Benjamin Banneker's
PENNSYLVANIA, DELAWARE, MARY-
LAND, AND VIRGINIA
ALMANAC,
FOR THE
YEAR of our LORD 1795;
Being the Third after Leap-Year.

PHILADELPHIA:
Printed for WILLIAM GIBBONS, Cherry Street

Banneker's almanac was very popular.

Banneker used a telescope to observe the sun, moon, planets, and stars.

COURAGE

9

Antonia Coello Novello (ahn-TOH-nee-uh coh-AY-yoh noh-VEL-oh) needed courage to overcome a difficulty. Novello was born with a serious illness. As a result, she was often in the hospital. She did not get the surgery she needed until she was eighteen years old.

At a young age, Novello decided to become a doctor. But her illness made going to school difficult. Despite her health problems, she went on to college and medical school. Later in her life, she was appointed United States Surgeon General.

In her government post, Novello worked to improve the health of all Americans.

It Takes Courage to Stand Up for What You Believe

Jane Goodall needed courage to stand up for an important issue. Goodall went into the wild forest of East Africa in 1960. She was a volunteer with little training in science but with great interest in chimpanzees.

Up to that point, many scientists did not think animals had different personalities. But Goodall believed differently. She gave the chimps she studied names, not numbers. She also took detailed notes about their personalities. Experts did not take her work seriously at first, but she believed in her method. Today, Goodall is a respected expert on chimpanzee behavior.

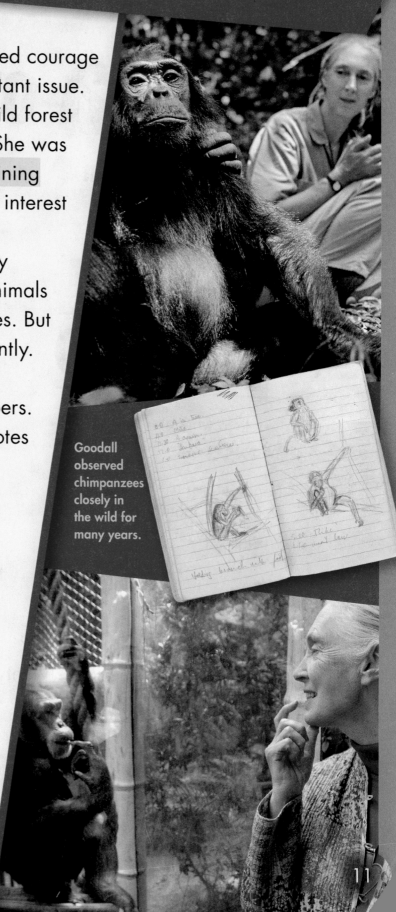

Goodall observed chimpanzees closely in the wild for many years.

Shipwreck in a Sea of Ice

by Sven Johnson

Shackleton believed "By endurance we conquer."

WANTED

People to work at a dangerous job with low pay and long hours.

Candidates must be prepared to work for months with not a single day off.

What if you read an ad like this? Would you sign up for the job? Twenty-seven men did. In 1914, they joined explorer Ernest Shackleton on a bold adventure to Antarctica, a land of snow and ice.

For power, *Endurance* had sails and a steam engine.

Traveling over the ice required sled dogs and sleds.

There were twenty-seven men in Shackleton's crew.

Shackleton and his crew traveled to Antarctica in a wooden sailing ship called *Endurance*. Their goal was to cross the icy continent on foot. No other explorer had done this.

The trip would be a challenge. But the crew was tough. Some had training as sailors. Some were scientists seeking knowledge. They would make detailed observations about Antarctica's land and weather. There were also sixty-nine sled dogs. They would haul both men and supplies.

COURAGE

13

The men played soccer for exercise while their ship sat in the ice.

The dogs stayed warm in igloos.

Endurance sailed in the Weddell Sea near Antarctica. Ice and storms made the sea very dangerous. But *Endurance* was a strong ship. For a month, it plowed through floating chunks of ice in the sea. But the ice pieces got larger and larger. They pushed against the ship and trapped it! As Shackleton pondered his next move, the crew spent time on the ice. They built igloos to keep the dogs warm. For exercise, the men played soccer.

OCTOBER 1915

The men set up camp on the ice.

Shackleton realized that the ice would slowly crush the ship.

Shackleton soon realized that *Endurance* would not last much longer. The pack ice was slowly squeezing and crushing the ship's hull.* Finally, the hull cracked, and seawater rushed in. The men unloaded food and equipment from the ship, including three lifeboats. In low spirits, they set up camp on the ice. Shackleton knew his job now was to get his men home alive.

***hull** body of a ship

The sinking of the ship stranded the men on the ice. But that was not the only bad news. The camp was on ice that was drifting out to sea!

Shackleton ordered the men to march toward the nearest land. The dogs hauled the supplies. The men pulled the lifeboats on sleds. But the ice became hilly and the men and dogs and sleds could not pass. All they could do was make camp and wait for warmer weather.

Endurance sat in the ice for eleven months before finally sinking.

The men would need the lifeboats to make their escape from the ice.

APRIL 1916

When the ice began to break up, Shackleton decided to launch the boats. He saw that the crew's best chance of reaching safety was to try to get to tiny Elephant Island.

The weary crew set out into the ice-filled sea. The waves were rough and the winds were cold. Heavy ice built up on the boats and had to be chipped off. For seven days and nights, the crew rowed and drifted through dangerous waters. At last, they reached Elephant Island.

The journey to Elephant Island took seven days.

Shackleton and five men made the risky journey to get help at South Georgia Island.

The twenty-two men left behind waved good-bye to the rescue party.

The crew was now safe and had fresh water, but the island was deserted. Someone had to find help. Shackleton and five men set off in a boat for South Georgia Island. It was eight hundred miles away, but it had a whaling station with large ships.

The trip to South Georgia Island was hard. Everyone was thirsty and weak from lack of sleep. One night, they were terrified by a giant wave that nearly washed them away. Still, they pressed on. What bravery!

Back on Elephant Island, the twenty-two men left behind were doing their best to keep hope alive. Living in shelters made from two boats, they waited and wondered. Four months passed.

At last, as they sat eating a lunch of seaweed and seal soup, someone spotted a ship. It was Shackleton returning! Cheering, the men rushed to the water's edge. They knew then that they would all make it back alive.

The twenty-two men stayed in this small shelter for more than four months.

What Do You Think?

After *Endurance* sank, what steps did Shackleton and his men take to save themselves?

Local Hero

by Miriam D. Otting

illustrated by Leslie Harrington

Katrina Wilson had never thought of herself as brave. Bravery was Superman saving the Earth. It was astronauts training for space travel. It was her friend Ritchie Swogger zooming down Piper Hill on his bike at top speed.

Sometimes Katrina wished she could be brave in an everyday kind of way, such as when she had to talk in front of other people. That was something she always dreaded.

20

The thing Katrina
did enjoy was taking photographs.
Once, in a photo contest, she won first prize. Her
photo showed a sunflower growing out of a crack in
the sidewalk.

But today was a school day. As she sat in class,
her eyes wandered out the window. Something was
moving. It was a young deer! And it was heading
for the woods beyond the schoolyard.

After school, Katrina asked her dad to go with her to the woods. Of course she brought her camera. They walked quickly toward a little stream. And there it was. The little deer had come to get a drink.

Katrina smiled. But when she saw a pile of garbage next to the deer, her smile faded. Katrina looked at the splendid, large trees and the flowing stream. *Too bad people don't treat these woods better,* she thought.

As Katrina walked home, she kept on thinking. *If those woods weren't so messy, people would go there more. They'd get to enjoy the deer, the pretty stream, and the trees.* An idea was forming in her head. The next day, she began taking pictures, lots of pictures.

At school, Katrina showed her photographs to other students. She wanted to challenge them to help clean up the woods. She rounded up seven volunteers, including her friend Ritchie. Katrina's dad and her science teacher, Mr. Nimms, agreed to help too.

"We'll need a truck to take all the trash away," said Ritchie.

Then Mr. Nimms said, "Katrina, why don't you tell the town council about your plan? I think the council might provide a city truck and some shovels for this project."

Before she realized it, Katrina had agreed to share her knowledge and give a speech to the town council. She picked out twelve photographs, including the one of the deer, and used them to create a slide show. Then she worked on the main points of her talk—the reasons for cleaning up the woods.

- People can enjoy a quiet, natural place.
- In the woods, people can learn about plants and animals.
- Trees help keep the air clean.
- The animals need a place to live.
- Having nice, clean woods improves our town.

Two weeks later, Katrina and her dad went to the council meeting. As they took their seats in the small crowd, Katrina saw the stage where she would stand to give her talk. She was terrified. Feeling her throat getting tight, she took a deep breath and let it out.

"You're ready for this," her dad reminded her. It was true. She had practiced her talk a dozen times. And she had detailed notes to look at.

When it was her turn, Katrina walked to the front of the room. She was still nervous, but as she showed the first slide, she remembered what was most important. Her voice grew stronger.

As soon as she was done, the council took a vote. They would provide a truck, shovels, and even garbage bags! Katrina's dad gave her a hug. Then a woman in the crowd came over and shook Katrina's hand. "That took courage," the woman said. "You're a local hero now!"

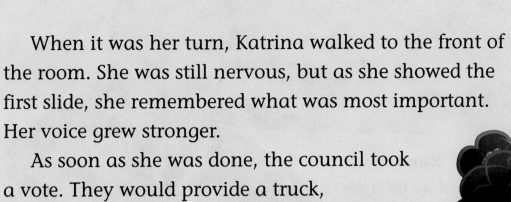

What Do You Think?

What steps did Katrina take to become a "local hero"?

Walt Disney was an American movie producer and pioneer in animated cartoons.

"All of our dreams can come true—if we have the courage to pursue them."
—Walt Disney

Speaking of Courage

DATE OF BIRTH	1901	1917
	Walt Disney	John F. Kennedy

John F. Kennedy was President from 1961 to 1963.

"We should not let our fears hold us back from pursuing our hopes."
—John F. Kennedy

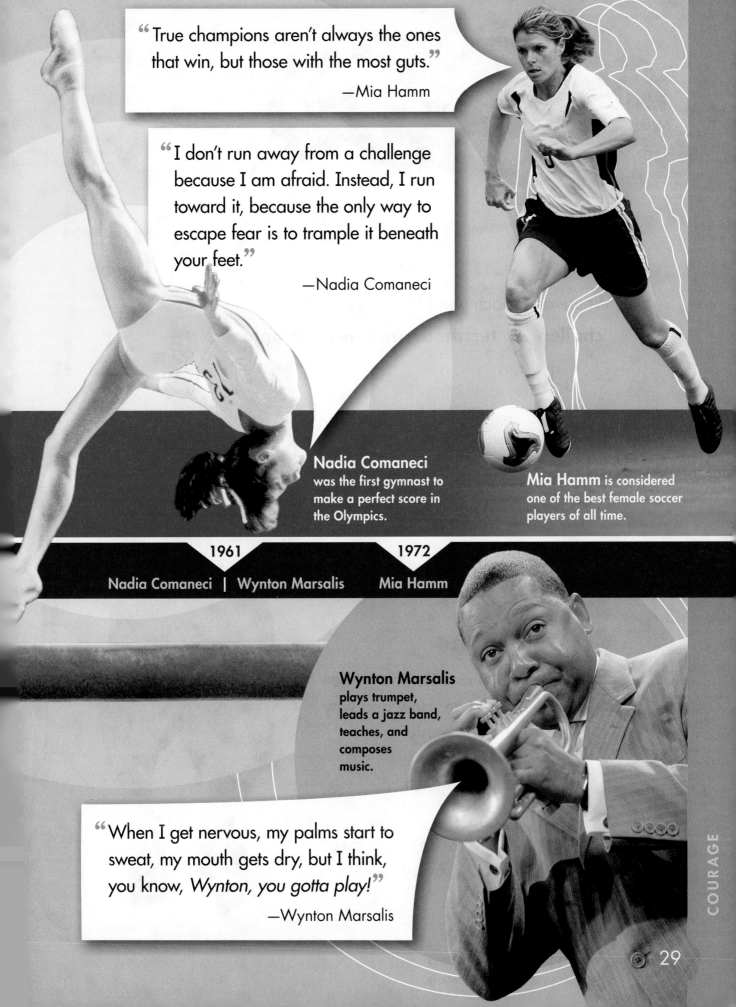

"True champions aren't always the ones that win, but those with the most guts."

—Mia Hamm

"I don't run away from a challenge because I am afraid. Instead, I run toward it, because the only way to escape fear is to trample it beneath your feet."

—Nadia Comaneci

Nadia Comaneci was the first gymnast to make a perfect score in the Olympics.

Mia Hamm is considered one of the best female soccer players of all time.

1961
1972

Nadia Comaneci | Wynton Marsalis | Mia Hamm

Wynton Marsalis plays trumpet, leads a jazz band, teaches, and composes music.

"When I get nervous, my palms start to sweat, my mouth gets dry, but I think, you know, *Wynton, you gotta play!*"

—Wynton Marsalis

COURAGE

4 YOU 2 Do

Word Play

Where does each word fit in the puzzle?

| challenge   terrified   training   volunteer |

```
          b
__  r  __ __ __ __ __ __ __
__ __  a __ __ __ __ __
          v __ __ __ __ __ __ __ __
__ __  e __ __ __ __ __ __
          r
          y
```

Making Connections

Ernest Shackleton and Katrina Wilson both showed courage. How and why did each act courageously?

On Paper

Write about a time when you showed or wanted to show bravery.

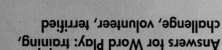

Contents

Natural Disasters

Words 2 the Wise

Natural disasters happen all the time. We can't prevent them, but we can learn what to do when they happen. As you read, think about what you know about natural disasters.

Natural Disasters

Nature can be wonderful. Tall mountains, colorful birds, and splashing waterfalls are examples of nature's beauty. But nature challenges us when a natural disaster strikes. Natural disasters are events such as earthquakes, forest fires, and storms. People do not cause natural disasters. But people are often the victims.

Tsunami waves can tower more than 100 feet high when they crash into land.

The 2004 tsunami nearly swallowed this entire community.

Natural disasters can cause great destruction. Think about the destruction caused by earthquakes, hurricanes, tornadoes, and forest fires. Earthquakes shake the earth. Buildings and bridges come tumbling down. Hurricanes and tornadoes bring strong winds and flooding. Huge waves called tsunamis (soo-NAH-meez) flood land. Forest fires destroy wildlife and homes.

During an earthquake, the earth moves suddenly, destroying buildings and roads.

Earthquakes can cause much damage.

35

This fire was caused by the 1994 earthquake in California.

In the 1930s, dust storms blew across an area of the Southwest and Great Plains of the United States. It became known as the Dust Bowl.

Many forest fires start when lightning strikes dry grass or trees during a storm.

Other natural disasters are less violent. But they are still destructive. Weeks without rain can cause a drought that dries up the earth. Crops cannot grow from this dry earth. Winds carry dirt off farmers' fields. The air becomes full of dust. Animals die of thirst because they cannot find water. Plants dry out and can catch fire more easily.

Think about a natural disaster you have seen or heard about. How did it change people's lives?

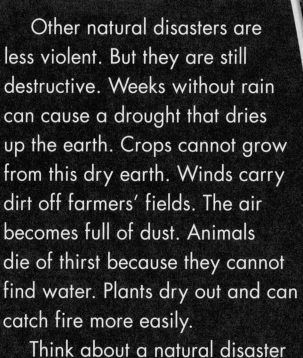

During a drought, a farmer's field turns into dry, cracked earth. Crops cannot grow.

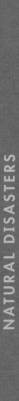

WARNING

Bugs at Work

BY GRANT PYTER

It's midday. You're sitting in a field, enjoying the warmth. Butterflies and bumblebees float above you. Ants and caterpillars crawl at your feet. Do you give these insects a second thought? Not really. They're harmless, right? Wrong! Insects may be small, but some can do gigantic damage. Millions of kinds of insects live in our world. Most of them are harmless. But a few can cause great destruction and disaster.

The Cycle of Cicadas

One example of those insects is the cicada (suh KAY duh). Cicadas hatch underground. They feed on tree roots. After 17 years one kind of cicada digs up to the surface. Millions of cicadas can crawl out at once. Scientists aren't sure why they are on an exact 17-year cycle.

People don't welcome cicadas. They do much damage. They are harmful to newly planted trees. Females make slits in the branches and lay their eggs inside. This weakens or kills young tree branches.

These branches have been damaged by cicadas.

Cicadas live most of their lives under the ground.

The Tiny Termite

The tiny termite can also cause mass destruction. Termites feed on wood. The wood they like to eat is in houses! Termites can tunnel through walls. No one knows they are there. Sometimes termites even eat carpets, plaster, and cloth.

These termites have made a pathway through the walls in a house!

Termites are true bookworms! They sometimes feed on a book's pages.

Most homes with termites may have three to four million termites!

Exterminators have found termites almost everywhere. They find them behind tiles in bathrooms and between stones in fireplaces. Sometimes they fly together in a big, black cloud.

It would be a disaster if homeowners ignored the signs of termites! Imagine a strong piece of wood. Then imagine how weak it would be if it were full of holes. Termites cause wood floors and walls to cave in. Sometimes they collapse.

Boll Weevils

The boll weevil (bohl WEE-vuhl) is tiny and destructive. Three of these insects might fit on a quarter. Female boll weevils lay eggs in the bud, or boll, of cotton plants. Young weevils feed on the plants. Adults also eat cotton plants.

Farmers can lose their entire crops to boll weevils! Farmers have ways to control boll weevils, and they have wiped them out in some places. The boll weevil is still the most destructive cotton pest in North America.

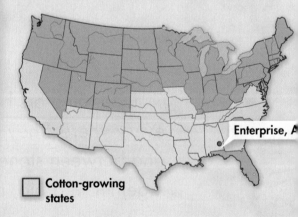

Enterprise, A

☐ Cotton-growing states

Boll weevils love to feast on cotton plants.

Boll weevils forced farmers to find new crops to grow.

Some good did come from the damage. Farmers realized that they could not depend on cotton. They found other crops to grow.

George Washington Carver helped introduce peanut crops to the region. Growing peanuts became a way for farmers to make a living. Peanut crops also helped the soil recover.

In 1919 the people of Enterprise, Alabama, designed and built a statue to honor the boll weevil. This town now calls itself "The Weevil City."

This statue in Enterprise, Alabama, honors the boll weevil.

The boll weevil is not the only insect that has taught us important lessons. Termites can almost tear down a whole house. But they can also make soil healthier.

People have even designed a way to honor termites. The Towering Termite is a giant model of the tiny insect. This gigantic model has been included in an exhibition. It teaches us about termites.

Termites work together to repair their home.

The towering termite is 69,000 times the size of a real termite!

Cicadas are known to completely cover trees and the ground in some places.

No monument or statue exists to honor cicadas. However, these insects can also be helpful. They dig holes which help air and water spread through the soil. This helps keep soil healthy.

Dead cicadas fertilize the soil. And trees nibbled by cicadas may produce more fruit the following season.

Insects are here to stay. It's up to us to learn how to live with them.

What Do You Think?

How can people learn to live with destructive insects?

45

AFTER THE STORM

by Patricia Curtis Pfitsch
illustrated by Fred Willingham

Elisa stared at her neighborhood. How could one hurricane have caused so much damage? Trees had fallen onto houses. Windows were broken. Clothes, toys, and furniture were scattered. People's belongings were everywhere.

Elisa stood in front of her house with her back turned. She slowly turned around. A branch of the big oak tree had landed on the front lawn. Her swing was pinned underneath. It did not look like the home she knew.

"Elisa," said Mama, "the important thing is that we survived. Watch Brian while I check the house."

"Can Brian go to day-care?" Elisa pleaded. Elisa and her friend Yuen had plans to see the baseball field.

"Elisa, the hurricane destroyed the day-care center," Mama said. "Who knows when the owners will design and construct a new building. Stay here with Brian. Don't go near the river. It's dangerous."

"Yes, Mama," Elisa said as she waved to Yuen.

Yuen sadly showed his muddy baseball mitt to Elisa. "Did you know that the baseball field is underwater?" Yuen asked.

"It's not fair!" Elisa was almost crying. "We practiced all summer, but now we can't go to the playoffs!"

Suddenly Elisa saw Brian walking to the back of the house. "Brian!" she called. "Stop!"

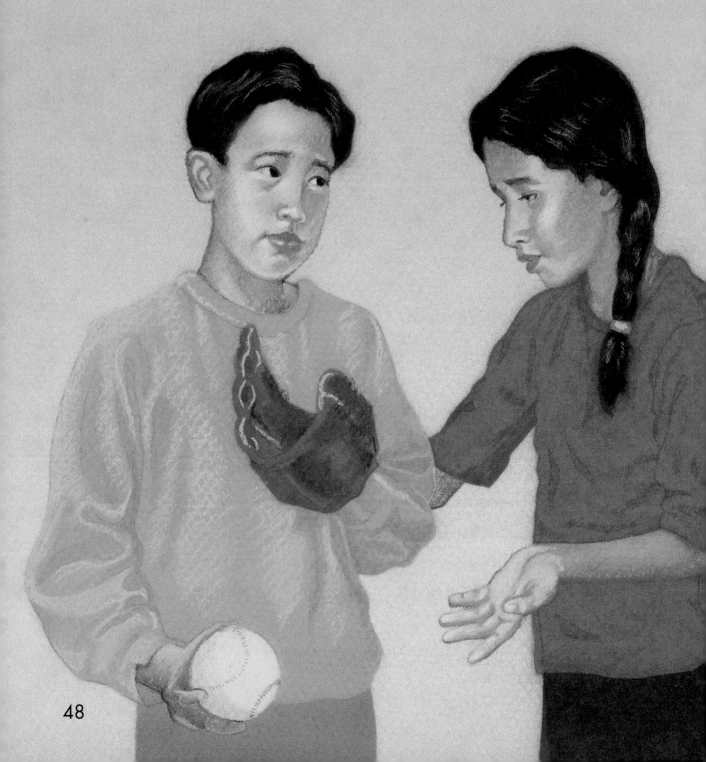

Elisa and Yuen followed Brian. Yuen told Elisa that he had to return to the motel. Elisa was going to stay at the same motel with the other survivors.

They caught up with Brian. "If the river hadn't flooded, Brian would be at day-care," she said. "Then I could pitch in the baseball playoffs."

"I have to go, Elisa. I'll see you later," said Yuen.

"What will happen to our houses, Elisa?" Brian asked.

"You mean our *house*, Brian," she corrected him.

"No," Brian replied. "I mean all the houses in our neighborhood."

The baseball playoffs faded from Elisa's thoughts. The hurricane had not happened just to her. It had happened to all of her neighbors.

She held Brian's hand as she stepped in the front door. The house smelled wet and moldy. The carpets and furniture were soaked. The rooms seemed dark and unfamiliar.

Mama gathered their undamaged belongings. Then, she noticed how sad Elisa looked. "What is the matter, Elisa?"

"I have been so selfish!" said Elisa. "I am so angry. Brian helped me realize that our surviving is more important than the playoffs."

"Perfect!" exclaimed Mama. Elisa and Brian looked confused. "That anger will motivate you to make great changes in this community," said Mama.

They returned to the motel and made plans to reconstruct their neighborhood. Brian would get kids together to clean up the park. Elisa would learn first aid to help injured people. Their neighbor, Mr. Harris, had worked on construction sites with other architects. Elisa would ask him to help start designing new buildings.

Mama invited the neighbors together to discuss their improvement plans. They made a list of materials they would need. They organized themselves into different groups, but they would all work together to rebuild their community.

"I am proud of you," Mama said. "Imagine how proud everyone will be to see our new community!"

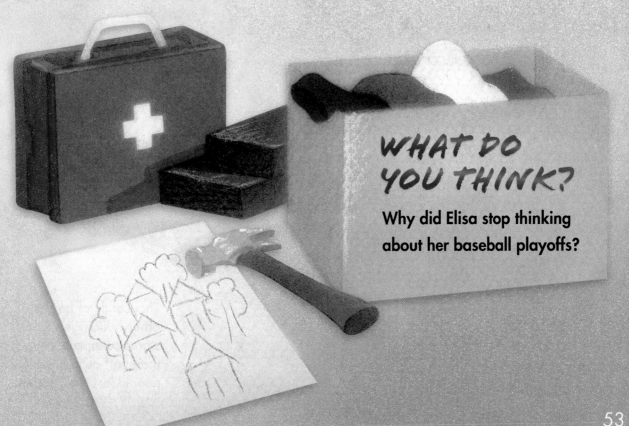

WHAT DO YOU THINK?

Why did Elisa stop thinking about her baseball playoffs?

At 5:13 a.m. on April 18, 1906, a huge earthquake shook San Francisco, California. The shaking lasted less than two minutes. This natural disaster destroyed much of the city. Hundreds of people lost their lives.

Scientists studied the earthquake of 1906 and learned much. Now we know more about how to detect earthquakes. Residents can be warned and take shelter. Today, there is less destruction from earthquakes.

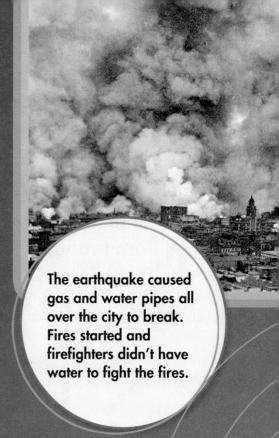

The earthquake caused gas and water pipes all over the city to break. Fires started and firefighters didn't have water to fight the fires.

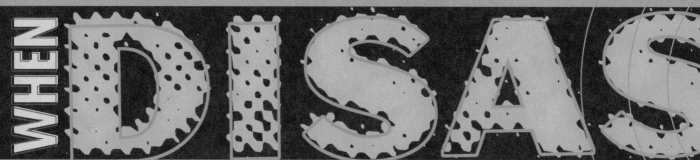

WHEN DISAS

The California earthquake of 1906 created a crack called a rupture, stretching 290 miles. That's about the same length as 5,100 football fields!

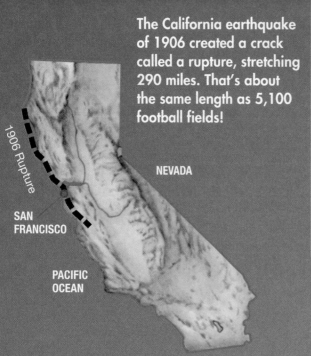

1906 Rupture

NEVADA

SAN FRANCISCO

PACIFIC OCEAN

Thousands of homes, office buildings, and stores collapsed. More than half of San Francisco's people lost their homes.

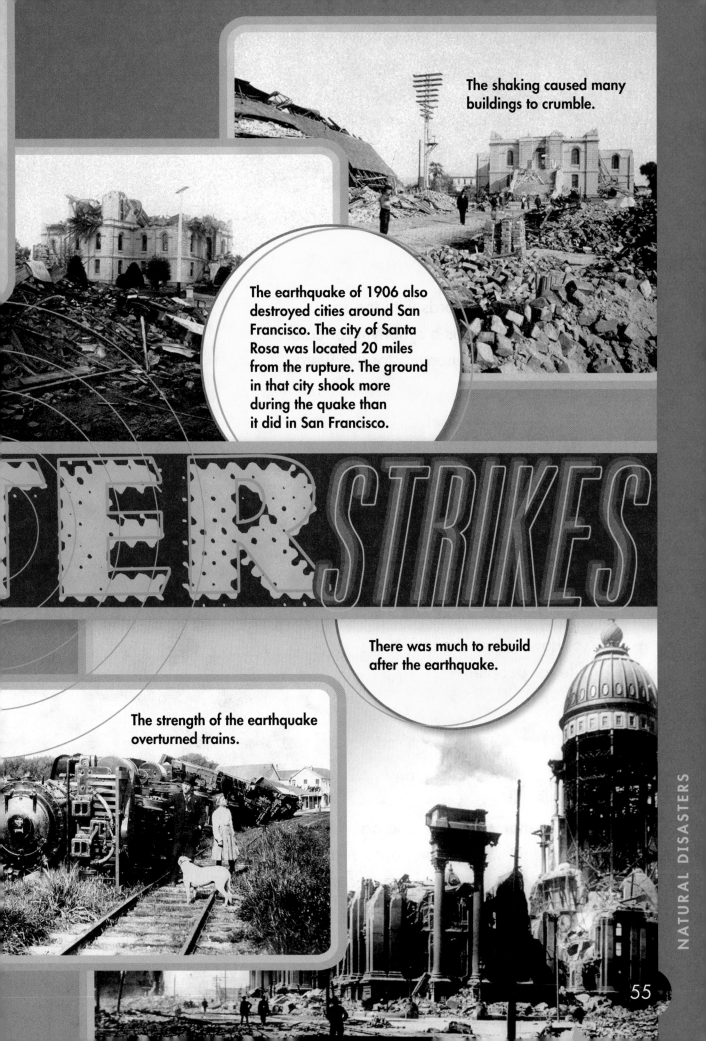

The shaking caused many buildings to crumble.

The earthquake of 1906 also destroyed cities around San Francisco. The city of Santa Rosa was located 20 miles from the rupture. The ground in that city shook more during the quake than it did in San Francisco.

TER STRIKES

There was much to rebuild after the earthquake.

The strength of the earthquake overturned trains.

4 YOU 2 DO

Word Play

Synonyms are words with the same meaning. *Chilly* is a synonym for *cold*. Think of three synonyms for this word: **damage**

Making Connections

Nature, such as insects and storms, causes life to change. The hurricane changed Elisa's life. What are examples of how nature changes life for people?

On Paper

Scientists, firefighters, and medical workers are some of the many workers who do important work before, during, and after a disaster. What job or career would you choose that could help in a disaster? Why?

Possible answers for Word Play: harm, destruction, ruin

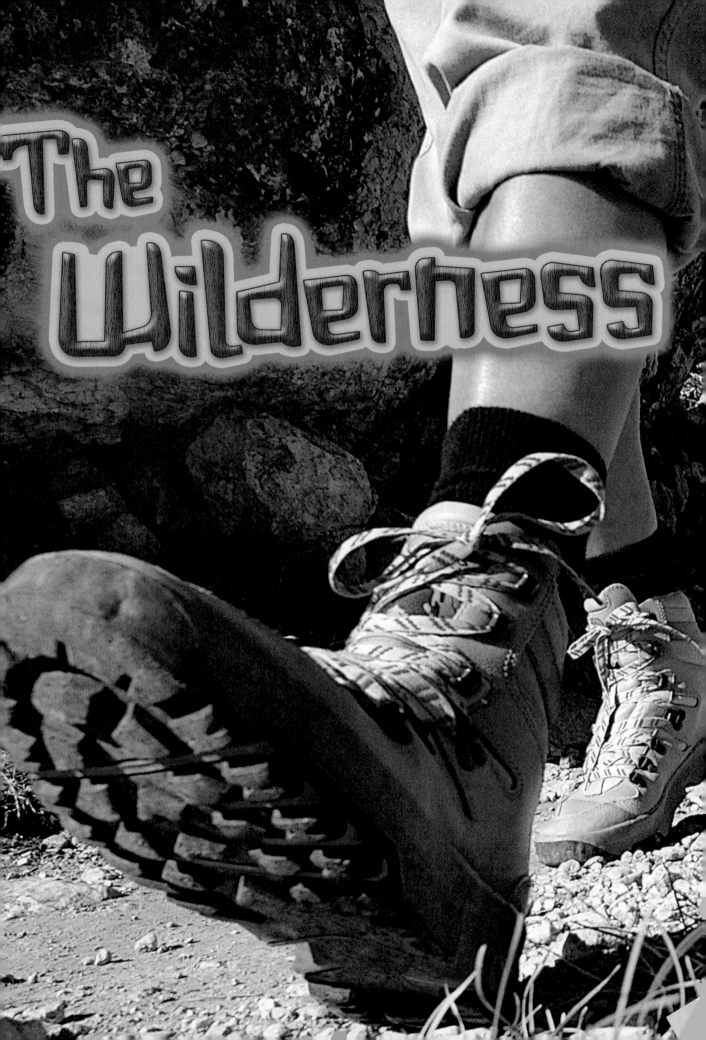

The Wilderness

Contents

The Wilderness

Words 2 the Wise

The wilderness is indeed a wild place! As you read, think about what you need to know before exploring **the wilderness.**

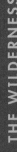

The Wilderness

Most people live in cities or towns. They live in houses or apartments. We turn on the heater when it's cold, and we turn on a fan when it's hot. People buy food in stores or restaurants.

Skiing is a great way to explore and enjoy the wilderness.

Many people like to camp in the wilderness.

Water for drinking, cooking, and cleaning comes from faucets. We are used to these comforts and expect them to be handy always. Some people like to leave these comforts and visit the wilderness.

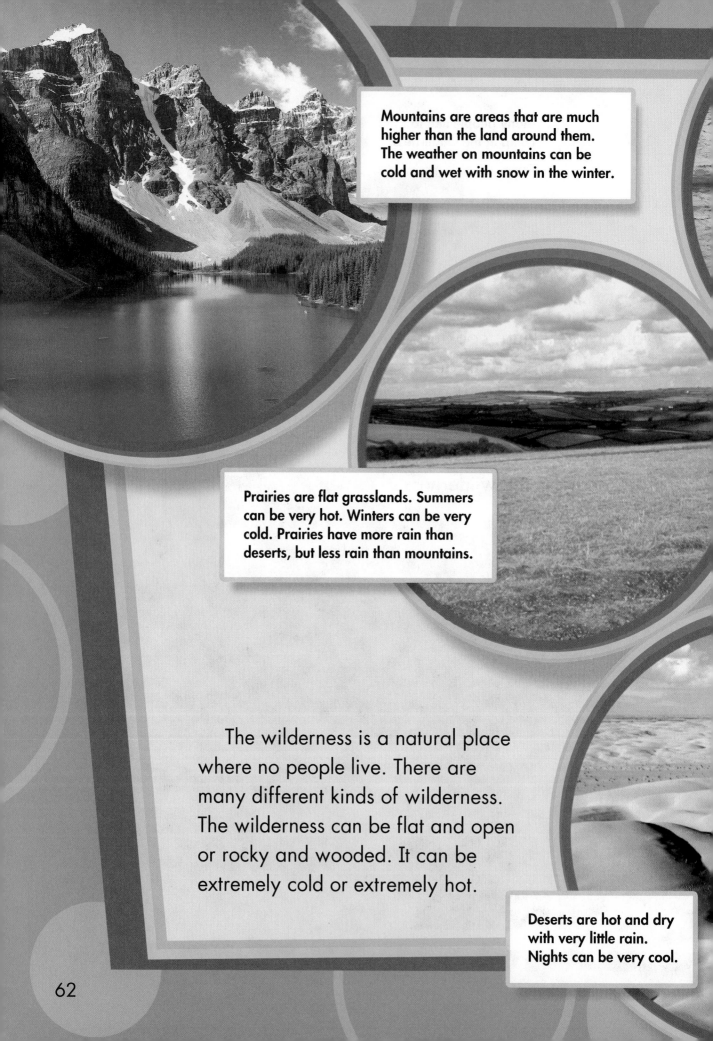

Mountains are areas that are much higher than the land around them. The weather on mountains can be cold and wet with snow in the winter.

Prairies are flat grasslands. Summers can be very hot. Winters can be very cold. Prairies have more rain than deserts, but less rain than mountains.

The wilderness is a natural place where no people live. There are many different kinds of wilderness. The wilderness can be flat and open or rocky and wooded. It can be extremely cold or extremely hot.

Deserts are hot and dry with very little rain. Nights can be very cool.

The Arctic is made up of water around the North Pole of the Earth. It is so cold that it stays frozen much of the year.

Forests are land covered with trees, shrubs, mosses, flowers, streams, and lakes. Many different kinds of animals live in the forest.

Look at these examples of different kinds of wilderness. Think about why most people don't live in these places. What are some challenges people might face when visiting each type of environment?

SURVIVING in the WILDERNESS

BY SUSAN MONTGOMERY

Aron Ralston chose to cut off his arm to survive after a rock-climbing accident.

BETWEEN A ROCK AND A HARD PLACE

Aron Ralston was hiking alone. He was in the Canyonlands National Park in Utah. He had not told anyone where he was going. A tragic accident happened. Aron was climbing in Blue John Canyon. A boulder came loose. It rolled into the narrow opening. The boulder crushed and trapped part of his right arm.

Aron was very experienced in wilderness survival. He used his knowledge to stay alive for five days with few supplies.

ID
WY
NV
UTAH
CO
Canyonlands
National Park
AZ

Canyons are deep, rocky holes in the Earth. They can be enjoyable.
But they can also be dangerous.

Aron considered all of his choices for survival.
He could make loud noise. Perhaps he could send a
message somehow. Aron couldn't get his arm loose.
Aron knew that one choice was to cut off part of his
arm to free himself. Did he have the courage to do this
to survive? Aron wrote about this accident in his book.
The book is called *Between a Rock and a Hard Place.*

THE WILDERNESS ACT

President Johnson signed the Wilderness Act of 1964. Today it protects the wilderness areas in the United States. In the wilderness, wild plants grow and animals live freely. Humans are not allowed to disturb them.

Animals can roam freely in the wilderness because of the Wilderness Act of 1964.

WHAT DO PEOPLE NEED TO SURVIVE?

Early wilderness travelers included explorers, settlers, and native people. They had to know how to stay warm and find water and food. The methods they used helped them survive. Modern inventions have made traveling in the wilderness easier.

Native people used supplies around them to su

This man stops for a night's rest. But one false move could spell disaster.

People need warmth, food, and water to survive. The human body can't survive if it gets too cold. People who live in cool climates wear warm clothing. They heat their homes to stay warm. Humans can live longer without food than without water.

It is also important to know the environment. For example, is it hot and dry? Will there be snow? This information helps us be prepared. Let's compare some survival methods from the past and present.

SURVIVING IN THE WILDERNESS, THEN AND NOW

It is important to be prepared for the wilderness. The ways that people prepare have changed over time. In the past, people used what was nearby. They also made their supplies. Today, we can buy what we need. Take a look at the supplies people used to explore the wilderness long ago. Compare them to the supplies we use today.

	CLOTHING	STARTING A FIRE
THEN	<ul><li>wool clothes</li><li>animal hides</li><li>fur</li></ul>	<ul><li>flint struck against metal</li><li>magnifying glass</li></ul>
NOW	<ul><li>man-made materials</li><li>rain jackets</li><li>jeans</li></ul>	<ul><li>waterproof matches</li><li>lighters</li></ul>

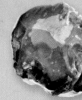

Flint is a very hard gray stone. It is made up of many tiny crystals of quartz.

WATERPROOF SAFETY MATCHES
Contents 45 matches•Strike On Box Only

It's important to be prepared for the wilderness.

FOOD AND WATER

- find edible plants
- fish or hunt for food
- draw water from streams or lakes

- freeze-dried or dried food
- Meals Ready to Eat
- edible plants
- fish or hunt for food
- bottled water

LOCATION

- trails
- using the sun and stars for finding directions
- compass
- maps

- detailed maps
- compass
- GPS

The Global Positioning System uses satellites to show where you are on Earth.

GETTING RESCUED

- signals
- fire
- mirror

- whistle
- mirror
- signals
- cell phones
- satellite phones

Being Prepared

The Seattle Mountaineers made a list called the Ten Essentials. These supplies will help people survive in the wilderness. What would you add to this list for different wilderness environments—the desert, the mountains, the forest?

Many people enjoy visiting the wilderness. New inventions have made it easier to enjoy these visits. It is important to learn the skills to survive before visiting the wilderness!

TEN ESSENTIALS
(Plus 1!)

1 Map and compass

2 Sun protection
(sunscreen, sunglasses, hat)

3 Extra clothing
(rain jacket and pants, poncho)

4 Flashlight
(spare batteries,
bulbs)

5 First-aid kit

6 Materials to start a fire
(matches, lighter)

7 Knife

8 Extra food

9 Extra water

10 Emergency shelter

Should there be an
eleventh essential?

11 Communication devices
(cell phone, two-way
radio, satellite phone)

WHAT DO YOU THINK?

What are some similarities between
past and present ways to survive
in the wilderness? What are some
differences?

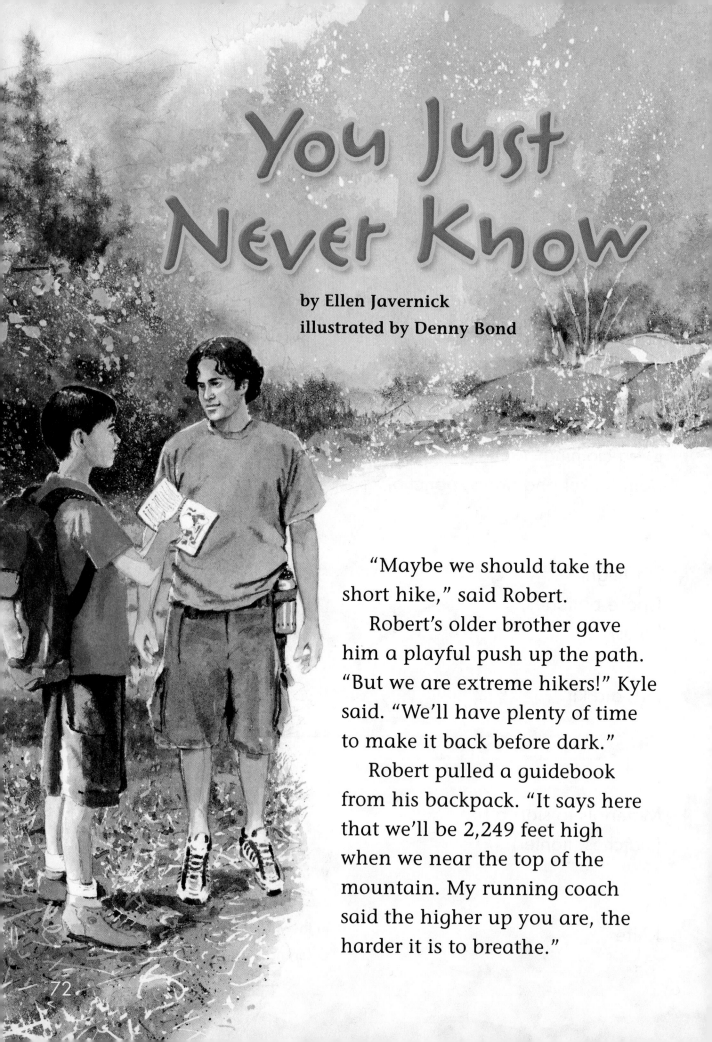

You Just Never Know

by Ellen Javernick
illustrated by Denny Bond

"Maybe we should take the short hike," said Robert.

Robert's older brother gave him a playful push up the path. "But we are extreme hikers!" Kyle said. "We'll have plenty of time to make it back before dark."

Robert pulled a guidebook from his backpack. "It says here that we'll be 2,249 feet high when we near the top of the mountain. My running coach said the higher up you are, the harder it is to breathe."

"I'm in good shape. Remember, I'm the star player on the North State College football team," Kyle bragged.

"I hope you're right, *Star*," said Robert. "Let's just keep heading north." Robert pulled his compass from his pocket.

"Wait. Let's go east on this trail," teased Kyle. "Your backpack is so full! Are you going to be in the wilderness for a month?"

"You just never know what you'll need," advised Robert. "I prepared for survival."

Robert looked at his compass and frowned. "Are you sure we shouldn't go to Eli Lake instead?"

Kyle agreed. They both turned onto the trail to Eli Lake.

The trail flattened out, but it was extremely rocky. Robert bounded ahead over the boulders. "You look like a mountain goat," Kyle called from behind.

Robert turned around just in time to see his brother slip. He ran back. Kyle's leg was badly gashed from the rocks and his ankle began to swell.

"I'm a little dizzy," Kyle muttered. Robert had to think for both of them. He grabbed the cell phone from his backpack and frowned. The battery was low.

"Kyle," said Robert, "I'm going to go ahead on the trail a short way to use the phone."

"Good luck," muttered Kyle.

Robert dialed 911. There was an answer. "We need help," he said. "We're in Big Mountain National Park. We hiked east from the sign to Eli Lake, and my brother's hurt, I think . . . Hello?"

Then the battery ran out. "I don't even know if they got my whole message," he told Kyle when he returned. "But when we don't show up at the ranger's office tonight, they'll search for us."

"I didn't stop to tell anyone where we were going," Kyle groaned.

"So now we have to stay in the wilderness all night?" squeaked Robert. "I'm going to search for help!"

"No!" Kyle protested. "I can't let you go alone. If you wait, someone will surely hike this way."

It was getting cold so Robert gave Kyle a thin blanket from the backpack.

"My little brother is taking care of *me*," Kyle said.

"Mom gave me some MREs," Robert said. "That stands for Meals Ready to Eat."

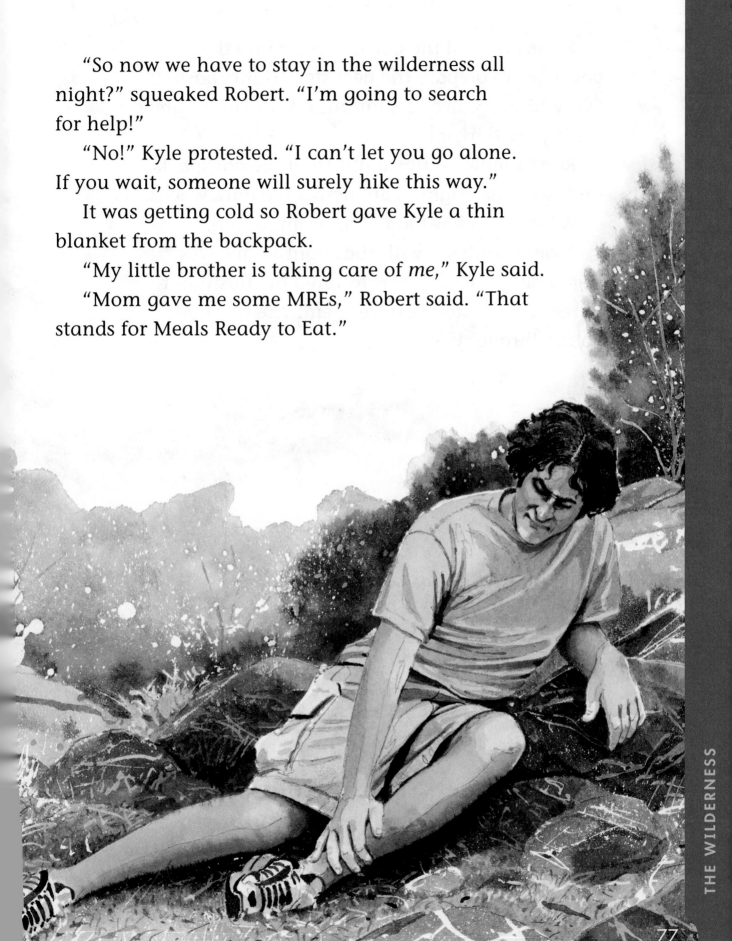

Robert poured the bottled water into the packages to prepare the beef stew. Hours passed. Everything seemed less familiar as the night grew colder and darker.

Robert pulled a flashlight from the backpack and swept its bright beam across the dark woods.

A large shadow loomed in front of him.

"Son, I can't see with that light in my eyes," said a deep voice. Robert lowered the flashlight. Three rangers stood above them. The call had gotten through!

"This is my brother Robert," bragged Kyle to the rangers. "He's a survival champion!"

Kyle leaned on Robert and wobbled as he stood up. "I said you were prepared to stay a month," Kyle recalled. "Who knew we'd need everything in your backpack for just one night!"

What Do You Think?

How are Robert's and Kyle's attitudes about the hike different? How do you know?

WILDERNESS
Survival Skills

Make a Needle-Nose Compass

1 Magnetize a needle by stroking it with a magnet.

2 Tie a twelve-inch piece of thread around the middle of the needle.

3 Hold the thread at the top end with the needle hanging at the bottom end. The magnetized end of the needle should point north.

Make a Solar Water Collector

1 Dig a round hole about three feet deep and three feet wide. Put a pan in the center of the hole.

2 Cover the hole and pan with a clear plastic sheet. Put dirt and rocks around the edges to hold the plastic in place.

3 Place a larger rock in the center of the plastic sheet to weigh it down.

4 In 24 hours there should be about 18 ounces of water in the pan. If it rains, it will also collect rainwater. The water will also be safe to drink because of this process!

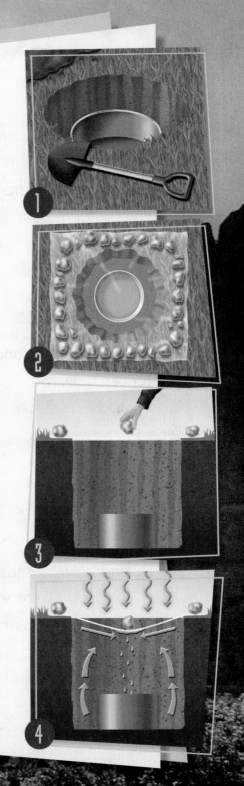

THE WILDERNESS

4 You 2 Do

Word Play

What is the smaller word in **WILDERNESS**? Make 5 other words from the word *wilderness*.

Making Connections

What are similarities and differences between Aron Ralston's and Robert's experiences in the wilderness?

On Paper

Which kind of wilderness area would you most like to visit: Arctic, desert, forest, mountains, prairie? What supplies would you need to survive there? Explain your answer.

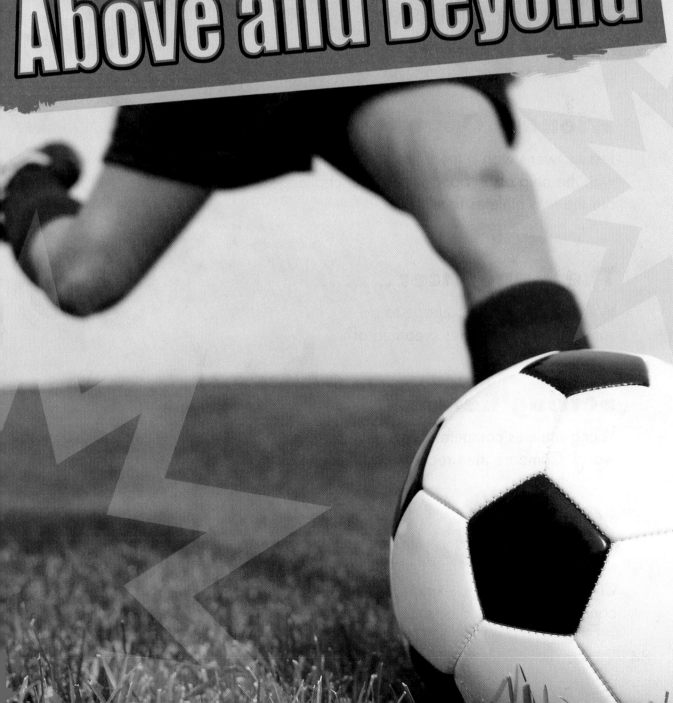

Above and Beyond

Contents

Above and Beyond

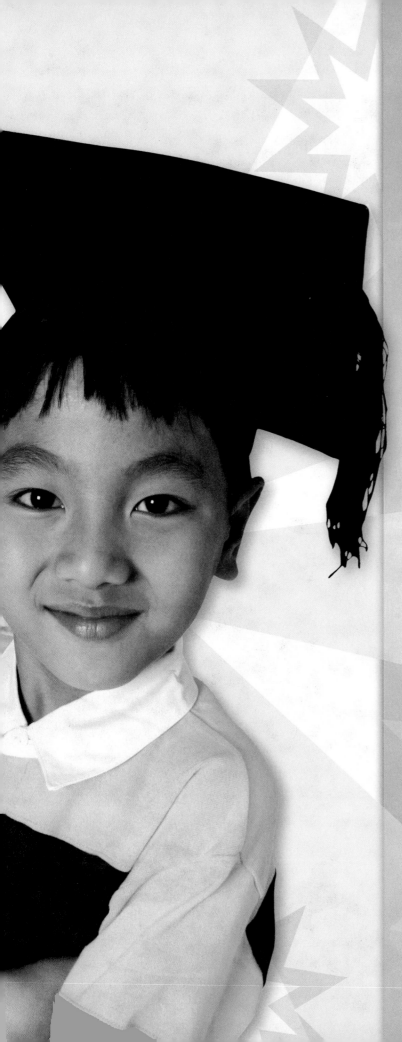

Words 2 the Wise

We go **above and beyond**, or triumph, when we do something we didn't think we could do. As you read, think about times you have triumphed.

Let's Explore

Triumphs

We face challenges every day.
Some are big. Some are small.
Some are fun. Some aren't
so fun. How can we triumph
when we face a challenge?

Try this: start small. Break the big problem down into smaller steps. Write the steps that you need to take. For example, passing a test might seem hard, but you can make it easier. First find out what you will be tested on. Then make a list of the topics. That way, you can study one topic each night.

Getting started is sometimes the hardest part. But the first step gives you confidence to go on. The next steps become easier. Remember, the first step in succeeding is to take the first step!

Ready!	Write the steps.
Set!	Plan which order you'll take the steps.
Go!	Act. Don't stop until you triumph!

Friendly OPPONE

By Tim Prentiss

Sometimes friendships between two people are surprising. This is the story of a friendship between two very different people, Jesse Owens and Luz (Lutz) Long. Jesse Owens was a famous U.S. athlete at the 1936 Olympic Games. Luz Long was a successful German athlete. These opponents would teach the world an important lesson.

Jesse Owens was a great track and field athlete.

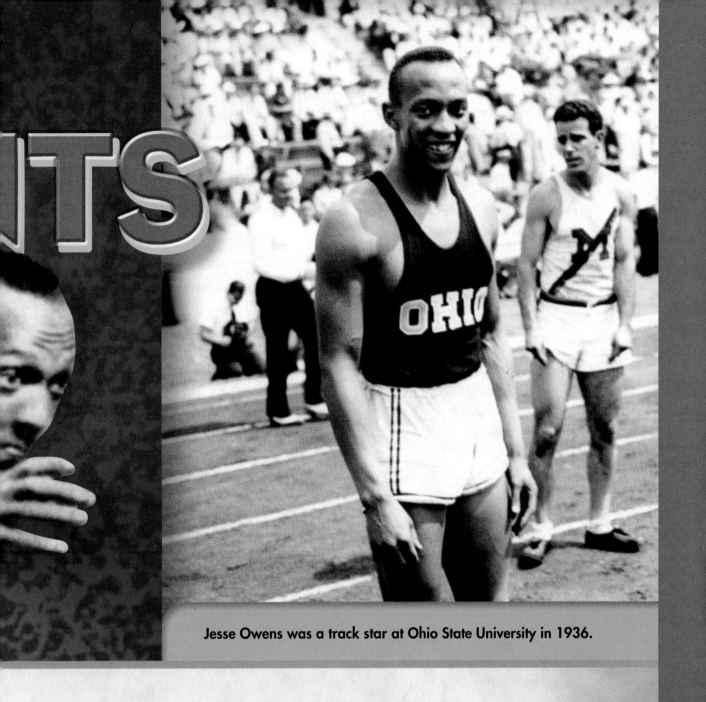

Jesse Owens was a track star at Ohio State University in 1936.

Jesse Owens was one of the most famous track and field stars in the world. He grew up in Ohio. Jesse was one of eleven children.

In 1933 Jesse was a high school athlete at the Interscholastic Championships at Soldier Field in Chicago. He won three events. Soon after, he set the world record in the 100-yard dash. Dozens of colleges wanted Jesse to join their teams. Jesse chose to go to Ohio State University.

In 1935, Jesse Owens became famous at the Big Ten Championships in Ann Arbor, Michigan. In 45 minutes, he set three world records. He also met one world record. He made a long jump of 26 feet, 8 inches. Nobody beat his record for 25 years!

Jesse Owens triumphed over some of the world's best athletes.

Luz Long was one of Germany's best athletes.

Adolf Hitler at the 1936 Olympics in Germany

The 1936 Olympics took place in Germany. At that time Adolf Hitler was the leader in Germany. Hitler believed that the German athletes were better than athletes from other countries. He expected his athletes to win more gold medals than other athletes.

Luz Long was a track and field athlete on the German team. Hitler expected Luz to beat Jesse Owens and win the gold medal in the long jump.

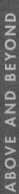

Jesse almost didn't get the chance to compete, though. He had to make a jump that was long enough so he could compete. Twice the judges told Jesse he had touched the foul line while launching himself into the air.

Jesse had only three chances to make the jump. If he touched the foul line for all three jumps, he wouldn't be able to compete. Jesse was worried. He had only one try left.

Jesse hoped his strength and power would allow him to compete.

Luz and Jesse became friends, even though many people thought it was wrong.

Before he made the last jump, Luz offered to help Jesse. Luz told Jesse to start his jump a foot before the foul line. That way, he would be sure not to touch the line.

Luz spoke with Jesse in front of everyone, including Adolf Hitler. Luz's bravery helped Jesse. It showed the world that not everyone believed what Hitler believed.

Jesse made the jump. He was able to compete! He won the gold medal with a jump of 26 feet, 5¼ inches. Unfortunately, Luz Long wasn't able to compete. His toe touched the foul line on all of his three tries. Jesse appreciated Luz's advice.

Luz congratulated Jesse near where Hitler was sitting. Both men knew that this displeased Hitler. But neither of them cared. They cared only about their friendship and competing in a sport they loved.

Jesse accepts his gold medal.

After the games, Jesse never saw Luz again. Luz was sent to Russia during World War II. He was killed fighting in Hitler's army. After his track and field days, Jesse traveled across the country. He talked to students about winning fairly.

Jesse learned from his opponent, Luz Long. Jesse said many years later, "The battles that count aren't the ones for gold medals. The struggles within yourself—the invisible, inevitable battles inside all of us—that's where it's at."

Jesse Owens used his talents to help others become better athletes.

What Do You Think?

What advice did Luz Long give Jesse Owens at the Olympics? What happened?

The Announcer

by Charlotte Clark
illustrated by John Sandford

Denise Jackson loved baseball. She loved the crack of the bat when it met the ball. She liked to smell the warm grass of the outfield.

Denise sat alone during baseball games. She spoke into a little gray box. She was recording a play-by-play of the game on her tape recorder. She pretended to be a famous sports announcer. Denise knew she'd never have the courage to speak in public, so she recorded herself instead.

Denise's father, Walt, knew she dreamed of being a sports announcer. He had taught her math using baseball scores. She conquered geography by learning where every baseball park was in the country.

One morning, Walt heard on the radio that Denise's favorite team was holding a contest. The winner would be an announcer for a spring training game. Walt bought a ticket for the contest that day. He couldn't believe it when the radio station called.

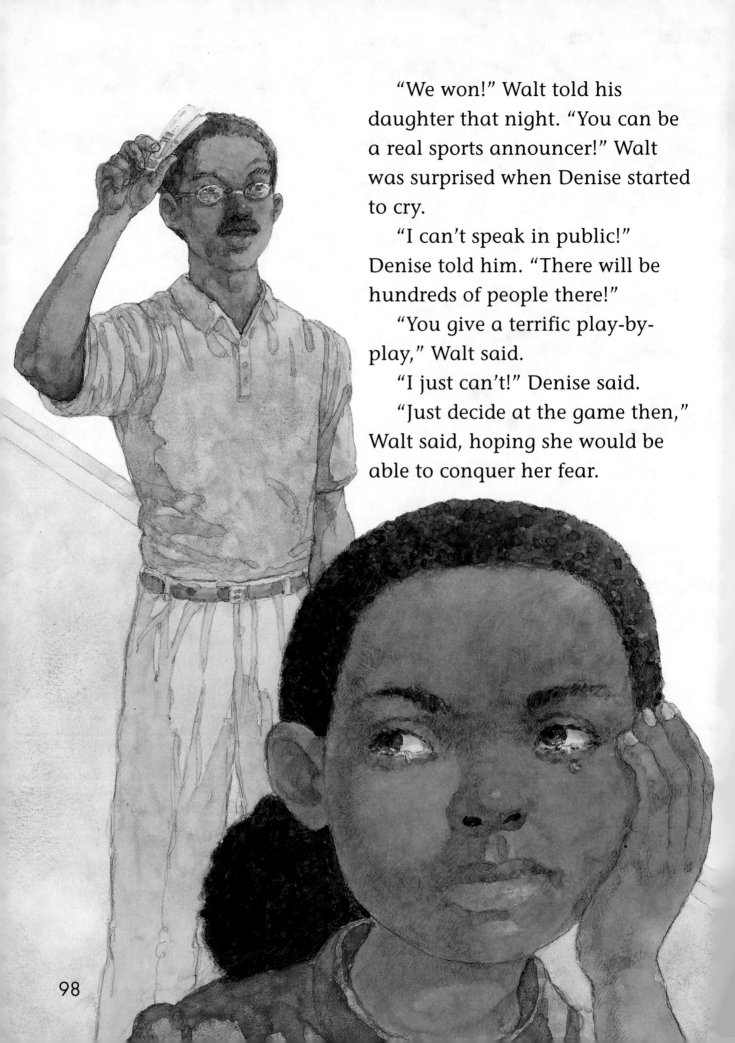

"We won!" Walt told his daughter that night. "You can be a real sports announcer!" Walt was surprised when Denise started to cry.

"I can't speak in public!" Denise told him. "There will be hundreds of people there!"

"You give a terrific play-by-play," Walt said.

"I just can't!" Denise said.

"Just decide at the game then," Walt said, hoping she would be able to conquer her fear.

For three days, Walt just smiled and nodded as Denise talked about the team. She knew every player's statistics. The day of the game, they walked excitedly into the baseball park. It smelled of grass, popcorn, and hot dogs. Denise pointed at her name, which was listed on the scoreboard as

"I can't do this, Daddy!" Denise said looking at the crowd. "Everyone will be staring at me!"

"But they won't even see you," Walt said. He pointed to a box high above them. "You'll be in there."

Denise looked up at the box and could hardly see the people inside. Denise knew he was right. But the challenge of announcing the game seemed scary.

"But, Dad, they'll *hear* me," Denise said. "My voice will sound terrible, and I'll forget the players' names."

"Denise, just listen to this," Walt said. He played Denise's tape recorder. She was describing a double play with a strong and clear voice. Walt stopped it.

"Denise, you know everything about baseball!" He put his arm around her shoulders and squeezed. "You've got to give it a try!"

101

The next thing Denise knew, they were standing in the announcer's box. Denise saw the equipment. She looked down at the field. Then she looked at her father. His eyes told her she could do this. She only had to find the courage within herself to take the first step.

When Denise walked into the box, a man helped her into her seat and handed her headphones.

"We start in two minutes," he said, smiling.

Denise heard someone talking in her headphones. It was the man next to her!

Denise saw her father behind him. It was time for her to talk. "This is Jenise Dackson, I mean Denise Jackson, your special announcer for the day." Denise's face felt as hot as the sun, and her heart pounded.

When the man looked at her again, Denise knew what to do. "Now batting," Denise said in a strong voice, "the left fielder, Steve West!"

What Do You Think?

What events lead to Denise's announcing the game?

Setting Records

Jesse Owens competed in four events in the 1936 Olympic Games, and he won four gold medals! Young athletes compete in the same types of events as Olympic athletes. How do these young athletes compare to Olympic athletes? As you look at the records, think about the challenges athletes face to be the best.

Jesse Owens making his record-setting long jump

You can test yourself against Jesse's winning jump. First measure 26 feet and 5¼ inches on the sidewalk with a yardstick. Then see how far you can jump from the starting point.

Athletes in a high jump must jump over a high bar without touching it.

High Jump

Olympic record (women)	6 feet 9 inches	Yelena Slesarenko, Russia	8/28/04
Junior Olympic Youth record (girls)	5 feet 7¼ inches	Sondra Biere, Des Moines, Iowa	7/27/90
Olympic record (men)	7 feet 10 inches	Charles Austin, USA	7/28/96
Junior Olympic Youth record (boys)	6 feet 4¼ inches	Grayson Galloway, Brevard, North Carolina	7/29/93

Javelin Throw

Olympic record (women)	237 feet 14 inches	Barbora Spotakova, Czech Republic	8/21/08
Junior Olympic Youth record (girls)	173 feet 6 inches	Hannah Carson, Mesa, Arizona	7/28/07
Olympic record (men)	297 feet 15 inches	Andreas Thorkildsen, Norway	8/23/08
Junior Olympic Youth record (boys)	184 feet 5 inches	David Reinhardt Bradford, Pennsylvania	7/25/08

In the javelin throw, athletes try to throw a pole as far as they can.

Runners must jump over hurdles in the 100-meter hurdle race.

100-Meter Hurdles

Olympic record (women)	12.37 seconds	Joanna Hayes, USA	8/24/04
Junior Olympic Youth record (girls)	13.85 seconds	Trinity Wilson, Oakland, California	7/27/08
Olympic record (men–110 meters)	12.87 seconds	Dayron Robles, Cuba	6/12/08
Junior Olympic Youth record (boys)	12.94 seconds	Tyrone Butterfield, Miami, Florida	7/28/91

4 YOU 2 DO

Word Play

Match these vocabulary words with the word or phrase that relates best.

athlete   tell

announce   opportunity

chance   Jesse Owens

Making Connections

Jesse Owens and Denise both had to face challenges. What challenge did each face? How did each one face the challenge?

On Paper

Jesse and Denise overcame challenges. Write the steps that you would take to overcome one of your challenges. Put them in order from hardest to easiest.

Life in a New Country

Contents

Life in a New Country

Words 2 the Wise

Life in a new country can be exciting and challenging. As you read, think about what it might mean to move to a new country.

Let's Explore
Immigra

It is one hundred years ago. You have arrived in America! You are nervous and happy. What will it be like? Will you find work? Will you be rich? Will you find freedom?

tion

Immigrants wait for the boat to take them from Ellis Island to New York City.

You are with many immigrants who feel just as you do. You arrive at Ellis Island in New York City or Angel Island in California. The immigrants are from many different countries and speak many languages. Some come to America to get away from war. Others come to live where there is more opportunity and to get jobs. You pass through inspection and enter the United States.

Chinese immigrants who were kept on Angel Island carved poems into the walls to express their feelings.

別客問如
此比除胎
挫西日吾

PASSPORT

United States of America

PASSPORT

PASSPORT

United States

However, some immigrants are not allowed to leave Ellis Island or Angel Island. Immigration officers decide that these newcomers are sick. Others do not have family or friends in the United States. These immigrants must stay in large buildings with small rooms. Some live there for many months, and some are sent back to their home countries.

All immigrants had to answer many questions and undergo a physical examination at Ellis Island.

Immigrants celebrate becoming U.S. citizens.

But you are among those who pass the tests. You go on to help shape the United States. You have many choices now. You and all the immigrants make America an interesting and exciting place to live!

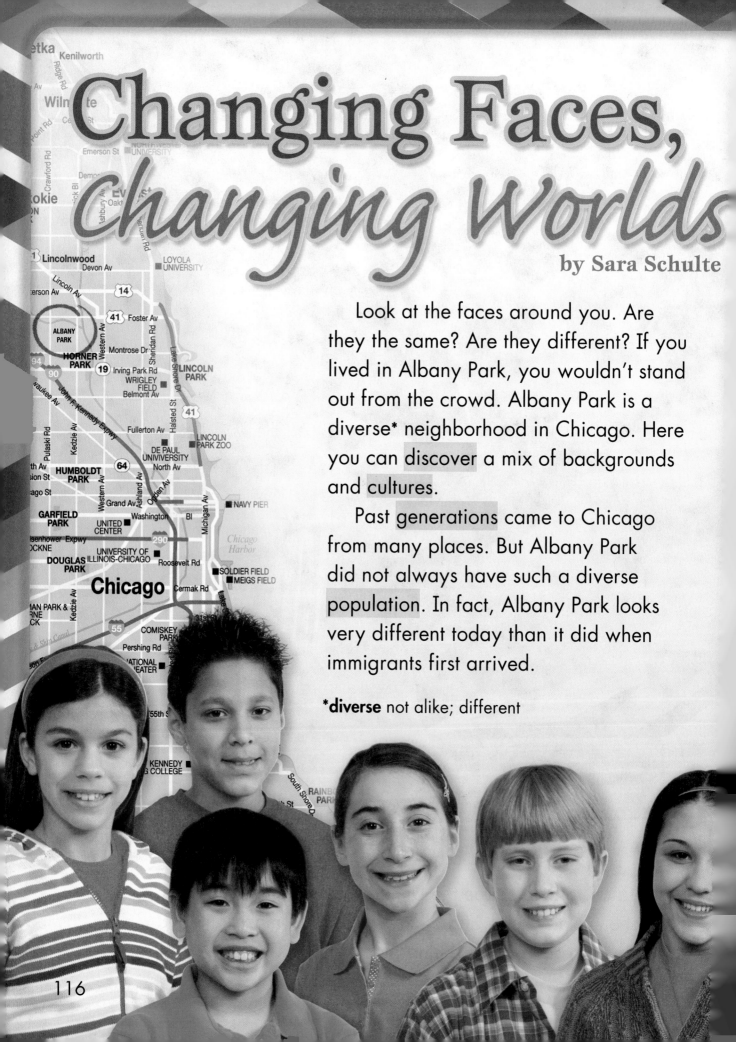

Changing Faces, Changing Worlds

by Sara Schulte

Look at the faces around you. Are they the same? Are they different? If you lived in Albany Park, you wouldn't stand out from the crowd. Albany Park is a diverse* neighborhood in Chicago. Here you can discover a mix of backgrounds and cultures.

Past generations came to Chicago from many places. But Albany Park did not always have such a diverse population. In fact, Albany Park looks very different today than it did when immigrants first arrived.

*diverse not alike; different

This cuckoo clock shows a German influence.

Some German immigrants were skilled craftsmen.

In 1868, German and Swedish immigrants settled in the area. Albany Park began as a farming community. But these settlers brought many businesses. German shopkeepers offered traditional leather footwear. They also sold handcrafted cuckoo clocks. Later, Germans began to make products that were nontraditional.

Germans also brought celebrations to Albany Park. The Von Steuben Parade happens every September. Von Steuben was a German who helped the Americans during the Revolutionary War.

Germans brought their traditional celebrations to Albany Park.

Swedish immigrants brought the art of dala painting to the United States.

Swedish families moved into Albany Park at the same time as the Germans. They brought fine crystal glass, dala painting,* and a kind of meal called smorgasbord.** The Swedish also brought printing and typesetting. Swedish newspapers printed in the United States reached Swedes all around the world.

Swedish men of Albany Park became laborers. Some of them built train cars. Others used their construction skills. They helped rebuild Chicago after the great fire in 1871.

*dala painting traditional Swedish painting using bright colors

**smorgasbord buffet with variety of foods

Swedish Covenant Hospital serves the Albany Park neighborhood.

Swedish immigrants brought the smorgasbord to the United States.

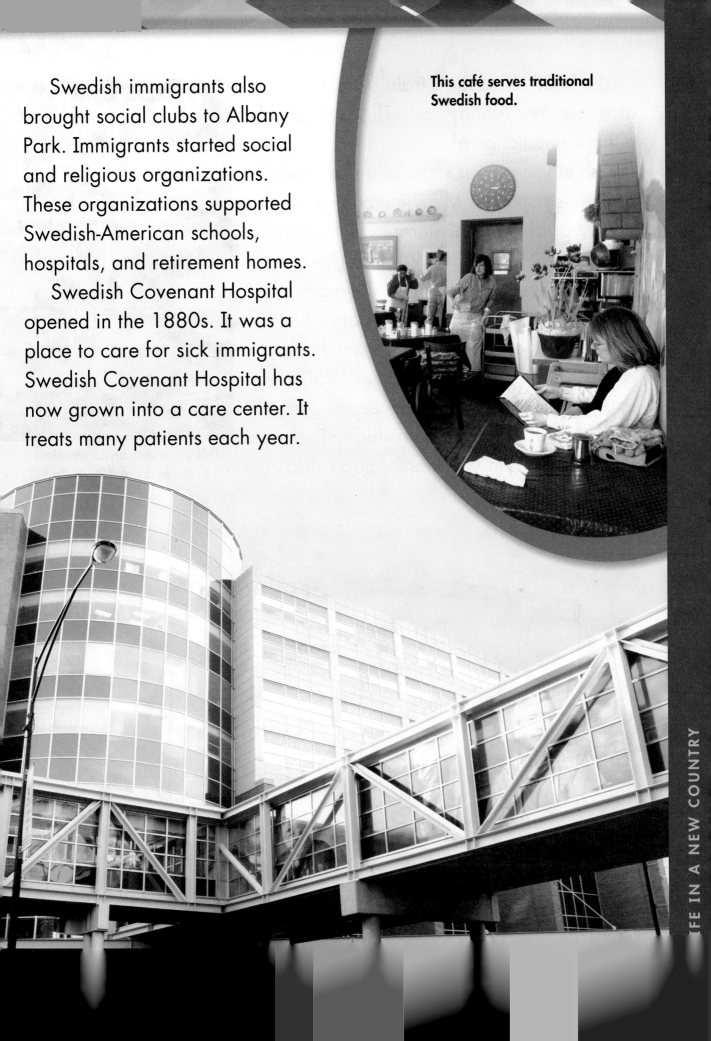

Swedish immigrants also brought social clubs to Albany Park. Immigrants started social and religious organizations. These organizations supported Swedish-American schools, hospitals, and retirement homes.

Swedish Covenant Hospital opened in the 1880s. It was a place to care for sick immigrants. Swedish Covenant Hospital has now grown into a care center. It treats many patients each year.

This café serves traditional Swedish food.

By 1907, Chicago's train system extended into Albany Park. This brought a large population of Russian Jews. Other Jewish ethnic groups soon followed. Jewish businesses opened. Many merchants lived behind or above their stores.

Between 1910 and 1940, the Jewish community built synagogues (SIN-a-gogs). They also started community organizations. They supported Jewish schools, medical centers, and public parks. In the 1950s and 1960s many Jewish families began to move. This big move left Albany Park in disrepair. Many businesses had to close.

This city train carries travelers into the heart of Albany Park.

This shows the center of Albany Park in the early 20th century.

In the late 1970s, Asian and Latin American immigrants came to Albany Park. They brought new businesses, food, and customs. Today, the Asian Food Grocery is an example. It shows the rebirth of Albany Park businesses.

Korean development has helped rebuild the Albany Park area. Korean newspapers, social service centers, churches, and volunteer organizations supported the new growth.

Dishes like these are served at Asian restaurants in Albany Park.

Lawrence Avenue in Chicago's Albany Park is home to many Korean-owned businesses.

Many signs are written in two languages to help recent immigrants.

There are many Korean influences on Seoul (sohl) Drive. Seoul Drive is a strip of businesses on Lawrence Avenue in Chicago's Albany Park. They are mostly Korean-owned. The community also has a Korean television station and radio station. It also prints two Korean newspapers.

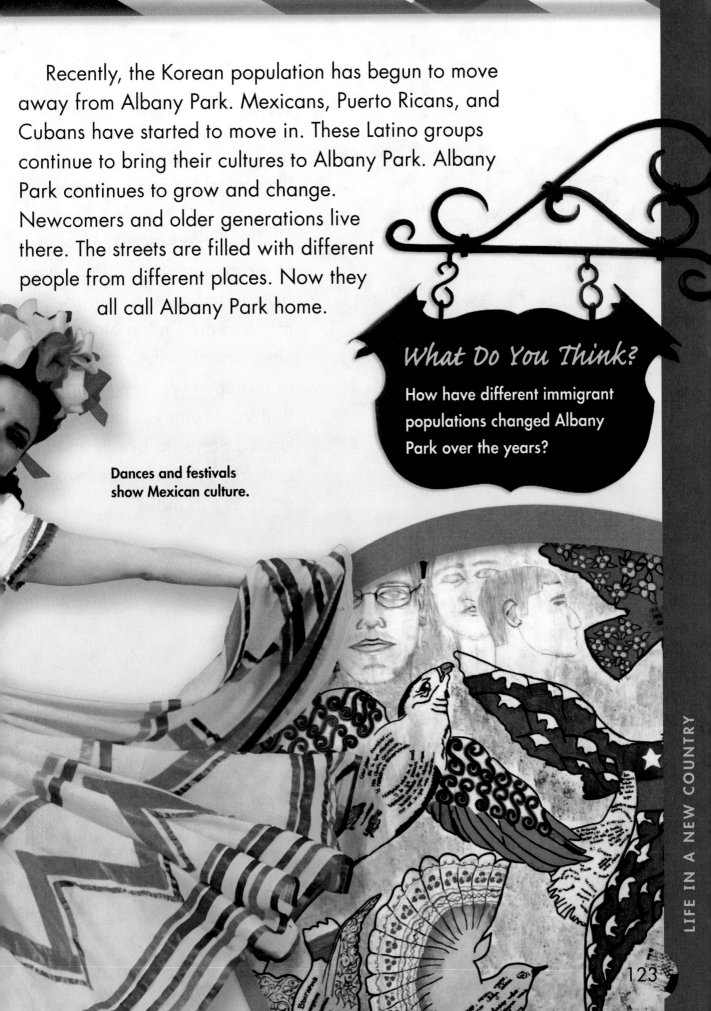

Recently, the Korean population has begun to move away from Albany Park. Mexicans, Puerto Ricans, and Cubans have started to move in. These Latino groups continue to bring their cultures to Albany Park. Albany Park continues to grow and change. Newcomers and older generations live there. The streets are filled with different people from different places. Now they all call Albany Park home.

Dances and festivals show Mexican culture.

What Do You Think?

How have different immigrant populations changed Albany Park over the years?

Farewell, U.S.A.

by Tim Prentiss
illustrated by Stacey Schuett

The United States is home to many immigrants. People from many other countries move to the United States. They adapt to the ways of life in this country. Now imagine that your family is leaving the United States to live in another country. What changes would you have to make?

People from the United States call moving to a different country "reverse immigration." They call it reverse immigration because it is the opposite of people moving here.

Why would people leave the United States? A person might move to Venezuela (vehn-ih-ZWAY-luh) to take a job as a mining engineer. Someone might marry a person from France and choose to live there. Someone might be interested in the country of their ancestry. They move back there to experience that culture.

A letter has arrived. Your mother has unexpected orders to work outside of the United States. You only have a few days or weeks to prepare to leave. Many children have this experience. There are nearly 250,000 American children living overseas, or in a different country. Kids can join some of the same clubs overseas as they can in the U.S.

Living in a new country gives you the chance to experience a new culture. You might wear a different style of clothing. Your house may be a different size. It may be made differently from what you are used to. You will probably eat different foods. You might also hear or use different languages. These new experiences could cause miscommunications!

You would have to make many choices to prepare for life in another country. What will you take? What will you leave behind? How do you say good-bye to friends?

Immigrants prepare for where they are going by learning the new language. They also study their new country's history and culture. They talk to other immigrants to learn how to prepare for the big move.

You must follow the rules of your new country. In the Netherlands, for example, all immigrants must report to the "Aliens Police." Alien is a word for a person who lives in one country but is still a citizen of his or her home country. Dutch law also requires everyone to carry an official identification (I.D.). Even small children must have an official I.D. at all times.

Another reason to go to a different country is to find out more about your ancestry. For example, a man from Germany moves to America in the early 20th century. 100 years later, his grandchild might return to Germany. The grandchild might want to learn more about the family in Germany.

Another girl moved to Indonesia with her family when she was three. Her family moved back to the United States when she was 15. Their experiences enriched their lives.

Moving to a new country is a challenge. At first, many things are unexpected. Newcomers might not have their "normal" routine. But soon, they become used to the new ways. In the end, they are proud to be a part of two cultures. They feel lucky to have friends around the world.

What Do You Think?

What are the challenges of leaving the United States and moving to a new country? What are the rewards?

What's in a Name?

See how some people get their names.

Some last names were based on land features that people might have lived near. For example, someone whose last name is Hill may have lived near a hill. Can you think of other names related to land features?

Some people were named by the type of work they did. For example, someone whose last name is Baker may have had a job baking bread. What job would someone have whose last name was Carpenter?

Family names told how children were related to their fathers. For example, Robert Peterson was the son of Peter. What are some other names that show children's relationship to their fathers?

Describing names tell about how a person looked. For example, a very strong person would have the last name Strong.

How did you get your name?

Cultural Naming Customs

- Some families name the firstborn son after the father.
- Some use nicknames because their real names should only be said on special occasions.
- People in Spanish-speaking countries often add the maiden name of the mother after the name of the father.
- Some African Americans in slavery chose a name used only within the family since the master chose their official names.

4 you 2 Do

Word Play

Reconnect the word parts to make real words.

non	ration
cul	cover
gene	ture
popu	traditional
dis	lation

Making Connections

How is a person leaving the United States like an immigrant coming to the United States?

On Paper

Look at a world map. Choose a country to which you would like to move. Pretend you are moving to that country. Tell why you chose it and how you feel about moving.

Answers to Word Play: nontraditional, culture, generation, population, discover.

an·ces·try (an′ ses′ trē), NOUN. your great-grandparents and all their parents before them: *Many early settlers in California had Spanish ancestry.* PL. **an·ces·tries.**

an·nounc·er (ə noun′ sər), NOUN. someone who describes sporting events or reads news on radio or TV: *The announcer gave the score of the football game.*

ath·lete (ath′ lēt′), NOUN. a person who has trained to be very good at a sport: *Athletes from all over the world take part in the Olympic Games.*

a	in hat	ō	in open	sh	in she
ā	in age	ȯ	in all	th	in thin
â	in care	ô	in order	ŦH	in then
ä	in far	oi	in oil	zh	in measure
e	in let	ou	in out	ə	=a in about
ē	in equal	u	in cup	ə	=e in taken
ėr	in term	u̇	in put	ə	=i in pencil
i	in it	ü	in rule	ə	=o in lemon
ī	in ice	ch	in child	ə	=u in circus
o	in hot	ng	in long		

be·long·ings (bi lȯng′ ingz), NOUN PL. things that someone owns; possessions: *I carry some of my belongings in a clear, plastic case.*

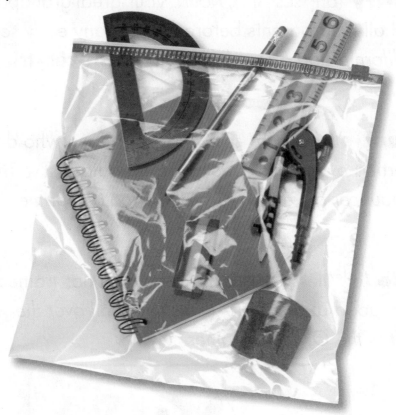

brav·er·y (brā′ vər ē), NOUN. courage; being brave: *The firefighters were honored for their bravery.*

chal·lenge (chal′ ənj),
1 NOUN. anything that tests your skills: *Fractions are a real challenge to me.*
2 VERB. to test your skill: *The duties of her job challenge her every day.* **chal·lenged, chal·leng·ing.**

chance (chans), *NOUN.*

    1 a good time to do something: *I had a chance to visit Washington, D.C.*

    2 a risk: *Mary took a chance and tried out for the school play.*

choice (chois), *NOUN.* something picked: *Her choice for the gift was a camera.* PL. **choic·es.**

com·pass (kum′ pəs), *NOUN.* an object with a magnetic needle that always points to the north: *She took her compass on the camping trip.* PL. **com·pass·es.**

com·pete (kəm pēt′), *VERB.* to try to win a contest: *Ben will compete in the five-mile run.* **com·pe·ted, com·pe·ting.**

a in hat	ō in open	sh in she
ā in age	ȯ in all	th in thin
â in care	ô in order	ŦH in then
ä in far	oi in oil	zh in measure
e in let	ou in out	ə =a in about
ē in equal	u in cup	ə =e in taken
ėr in term	u̇ in put	ə =i in pencil
i in it	ü in rule	ə =o in lemon
ī in ice	ch in child	ə =u in circus
o in hot	ng in long	

con·quer (kong′ kər), VERB. to overcome someone or something; to take over: *Jim had to conquer his shyness to be a good actor.* **con·quered, con·quer·ing.**

con·struct (kən strukt′), VERB. to put something together; to build: *Sam will construct a raft of logs held together with rope.* **con·struct·ed, con·struct·ing.**

cul·ture (kul′ chər), NOUN. a way of life; culture includes things like foods, celebrations, and languages: *In a big city, you can find people from many different cultures.* PL. **cul·tures.**

dam·age (dam′ ij), NOUN. harm or injury: *The accident caused some damage to the car.*

de·sign (di zīn′), VERB. to draw, plan, or sketch: *The architect will design the new apartment building.* **de·signed, de·sign·ing.**

de·struc·tion (di struk′ shən), *NOUN.* great damage:
There was much destruction after the hurricane.

de·tailed (di tāld or dē′ tāld), *ADJECTIVE.* full of details:
He gave a detailed account of his trip to Spain.

dis·as·ter (də zas′ tər), *NOUN.* a
sudden event that causes great
suffering or loss: *A flood, fire,
or earthquake is a disaster.*

dis·co·ver (dis kuv′ ər), *VERB.* to find
out something that was not known before: *People in a new
country can discover a different culture.* **dis·cov·ered,
dis·cov·er·ing.**

en·vi·ron·ment (en vī′ rən mənt), *NOUN.* everything that
surrounds a living thing: *In order to grow, plants need an
environment with enough light and water.*

a in hat	ō in open	sh in she
ā in age	ȯ in all	th in thin
â in care	ô in order	ŦH in then
ä in far	oi in oil	zh in measure
e in let	ou in out	ə =a in about
ē in equal	u in cup	ə =e in taken
ėr in term	u̇ in put	ə =i in pencil
i in it	ü in rule	ə =o in lemon
ī in ice	ch in child	ə =u in circus
o in hot	ng in long	

ex·per·i·ence (ek spir′ ē əns),

    1 *NOUN.* events that are seen, done, or lived through: *Sarah did not have a good experience living on the farm.*

    2 *VERB.* to have happen to you: *I can't wait to experience how it feels to ride a roller coaster.* **ex·per·i·enced, ex·per·i·en·cing.**

flint (flint), *NOUN.* a very hard stone that makes a spark when it is struck against metal: *We used flint to start our campfire.*

gen·e·ra·tion (jen′ ə rā′ shən), *NOUN.*

    groups of people born at about the same time: *You and your friends are from the same generation.* *PL.* **gen·e·ra·tions.**

knowl·edge (nol′ ij), *NOUN.* what you know: *Gardeners have a great knowledge of flowers.*

non·tra·di·tion·al (non trə dish′ ə nəl), *ADJECTIVE.* something that is not made or done according to customs or beliefs: *"Wheels on the Bus" is a nontraditional song to sing at a baseball game.*

op·po·nent (ə pō′ nənt), *NOUN.* someone who is on the other side in a fight or contest: *The two opponents competed in a race.* PL. **op·po·nents.**

pop·u·la·tion (pop′ yə lā′ shən), *NOUN.* the people of a city, country, or district: *The population of Chicago is made up of people from different countries.*

pre·pare (pri pâr′), *VERB.* to get ready: *They will prepare a big feast for the holiday.* **pre·pared, pre·par·ing.**

a in hat	ō in open	sh in she
ā in age	ȯ in all	th in thin
â in care	ô in order	ᴛH in then
ä in far	oi in oil	zh in measure
e in let	ou in out	ə =a in about
ē in equal	u in cup	ə =e in taken
ėr in term	u̇ in put	ə =i in pencil
i in it	ü in rule	ə =o in lemon
ī in ice	ch in child	ə =u in circus
o in hot	ng in long	

pub·lic (pub′ lik), NOUN. in view of other people: *The President spoke in public about his ideas to lower taxes.*

sup·plies (sə plīs′), NOUN PL. the food or equipment necessary for a trip: *Flashlights, compasses, and matches are important camping supplies.*

sur·vive (sər vīv′), VERB. to continue to live or exist; remain: *We need food and water to survive.* **sur·vived, sur·viv·ing.**

ter·mite (tėr′ mīt), NOUN. an insect with a soft, pale body that feeds on wood: *Termites can be very destructive to buildings.*

ter·ri·fied (ter′ ə fīd), ADJECTIVE. very afraid: *I was terrified of the huge dog.*

train·ing (trā′ ning), NOUN. special education for a job: *The President called for more training for teachers.*

un·ex·pect·ed (un′ ek spek′ tid), ADJECTIVE. by surprise: *We had an unexpected visit from our grandmother last week.*

vol·un·teer (vol′ ən tir′),

    1 *VERB.* to offer your services; to offer to help: *I volunteered for the job.* **vol·un·teered, vol·un·teer·ing.**

    2 *NOUN.* a person who works without pay: *I am a volunteer at the hospital.*

wil·der·ness (wil′ dər nis), *NOUN.* a wild place with few or no people living in it: *I want to explore the wilderness.*

a	in hat	ō	in open	sh	in she
ā	in age	ȯ	in all	th	in thin
â	in care	ô	in order	ŦH	in then
ä	in far	oi	in oil	zh	in measure
e	in let	ou	in out	ə	=a in about
ē	in equal	u	in cup	ə	=e in taken
ėr	in term	u̇	in put	ə	=i in pencil
i	in it	ü	in rule	ə	=o in lemon
ī	in ice	ch	in child	ə	=u in circus
o	in hot	ng	in long		

Acknowledgments

Illustrations

Cover: Denny Bond, Gary Torrisi; **3** Alan Flinn; **20–26** Leslie Harrington; **32, 46–53** Fred Willingham; **42, 54, 65** Susan J. Carlson; **58, 72–78** Denny Bond; **81** Rob Schuster; **84, 96–103** John Sandford; **110, 124–130** Stacey Schuett.

Photographs

Every effort has been made to secure permission and provide appropriate credit for photographic material. The publisher deeply regrets any omission and pledges to correct errors called to its attention in subsequent editions. Unless otherwise acknowledged, all photographs are the property of Pearson Education, Inc. Photo locators denoted as follows: Top (T), Center (C), Bottom (B), Left (L), Right (R), Background (Bkgd)

Cover: (BR) Popperfoto/Alamy Images, (Back) Stockdisc, (CR) USDA/Nature Source/Photo Researchers, Inc., (B) White Cross Productions/Getty Images; **1** (CL) White Cross Productions/Getty Images; **2** (CR) ©STAFF/AFP/Getty Images, (BR) USDA/Nature Source/Photo Researchers, Inc.; **3** (TC) Andy Crawford/DK Images, (CR) Bob Daemmrich/PhotoEdit, (BR) Stockdisc; **5** (C) ©Thomas Barwick/Getty Images; **6** (BR) ©Paul J. Sutton/Duomo/Corbis, (CR) ©Royal Geographical Society/Alamy Images, (C) ©The Granger Collection, NY; **7** (CL) ©moodboard/Corbis; **8** (C) ©Lon C. Diehl/PhotoEdit; **9** (C) ©The Granger Collection, NY, (B) Mount Vernon Ladies' Association; **10** (B) ©AP Photo, (C) ©Bob Daugherty/AP Images, (CL) ©Lori Martin/Shutterstock; **11** (T) ©/Getty Images, (CR) ©Michael Nichols/National Geographic Image Collection, (BR) Tim Ridley/Courtesy of the Jane Goodall Institute, Clarendon Park, Hampshire/©DK Images; **12** (C) ©Underwood & Underwood/Corbis; **13** (C) ©Royal Geographical Society/Alamy Images; **14** (C) ©Royal Geographical Society/Alamy Images, (C) ©Royal Georgraphical Society/Alamy Images; **15** (C) ©Royal Geographical Society/Alamy Images; **16** (C) ©Royal Geographical Society/Alamy Images; **17** (C) ©Royal Geographical Society/Alamy Images; **18** (C) ©Royal Geographical Society/Alamy Images; **19** (C) ©Royal Geographical Society/Alamy Images; **28** (TR) ©Bettmann/Corbis, (C) ©STAFF/AFP/Getty Images, (BC) Corbis; **29** (CR) ©Aguilar/Reuters/Corbis, (TR) ©Paul J. Sutton/Duomo/Corbis, (BL) ©STAFF/AFP/Getty Images; **30** (BR) ©moodboard/Corbis; **31** (Bkgd) Woodfall Wild Images/Alamy Images; **32** (TR) AP/Wide World Photos, (BR) U.S. Geological Survey, (CR) USDA/Nature Source/Photo Researchers, Inc.; **33** (L) Glen E. Ellman; **34** (BR) AP/Wide World Photos, (TR, BL) Getty Images, (TL) Reuters/Corbis; **35** (TL, BR, BL) AP/Wide World Photos, (TR) Getty Images; **36** (TR) American Stock/Getty Images, (TL) AP/Wide World Photos, (BL) Getty Images, (BR) John M. Roberts/Corbis; **37** (TR) Erik Rank/Getty Images, (TL, BR) Getty Images, (BL) Michael S. Lewis/Getty Images; **38** (B) Getty Images; **39** (L) Darlyne A. Murawski/Getty Images, (B) Getty Images, (BR) John Lemker/Animals Animals/Earth Scenes; **40** (BL) Bryan Mullennix/Getty Images, (CL) Fabio Colombini Medeiros/Animals Animals/Earth Scenes; **41** (B) Getty Images, (BL) Pascal Goetgheluck/Photo Researchers, Inc., (T) Steve Russell/Toronto Star/Zuma Press, Inc.; **42** (L) ©Nigel Caittlin/Alamy Images, (B) Getty Images; **43** (BR) AP/Wide World Photos, (T) USDA/Nature Source/Photo Researchers, Inc.; **44** (B) Photo courtesy of Termidor® Termite Defense™; **45** (TR) AP/Wide World Photos, (B) Getty Images, (TL) Peter Johnson/Corbis; **54** (TR) Bettmann/Corbis, (BR) U.S. Geological Survey; **55** (TR, TL) ©Courtesy of the Bancroft Library, University of California, Berkeley, (BR) Steinbrugge Collection/EERC/University of California, Berkeley, (BL) U.S. Geological Survey; **56** (BR) Glen E. Ellman; **57** (CC) Getty Images; **58** (TC, B) Getty Images, (BR) Library of Congress; **59** (TL, T, CR, CL, BR, BL) Getty Images, (L) White Cross Productions/Getty Images; **60** (CC, C) Getty Images, (BL) Tom Stewart/Corbis; **61** (BR) Hemera Technologies, (TR) Rob Gage/Getty Images; **62** (TL) ©Royalty-Free/Corbis, (BR) Craig Aurness/Corbis, (CR) ©Getty Images/Thinkstock; **63** (TR) Getty Images, (TL) Per Breiehagen/Getty Images, (CR) Theo Allofs/Getty Images; **64** (BL) AP/Wide World Photos, (TR) Getty Images; **65** (TR) Getty Images; **66** (TL, BR) Bettmann/Corbis, (TR) Gail Shumway/Getty Images, (BL) Getty Images; **67** (T) Gordon Wiltsie/Getty Images; **68** (C) Geoff Brightling, Courtesy of the Pitt Rivers Museum, University of Oxford/DK Images, (BC) Gerald Lopez/DK Images, (CR) Harry Taylor/DK Images; **69** (T) ©Royalty-Free/Corbis, (BL) Dave King/DK Images, (BR, BL) DK Images, (CL) Frank Greenway/DK Images, (C) Geoff Brightling/DK Images, (CR) Getty Images, (BC) Jeff Randall/Index Stock Imagery; **70** (B) Andy Crawford/DK Images, (TR) Getty Images, (BR) ©Purestock/Alamy; **71** (BL, BC) DK Images, (TL) Nicholas Eveleigh/Getty Images, (CL) Steve Gorton/DK Images; **80** (BR) Andy Crawford/DK Images, (TR, CC) Getty Images; **82** (TR) Getty Images, (CL) White Cross Productions/Getty Images; **83** Brand X Pictures; **84** (TR) Blend Images/Getty Images, (BR) Bob Daemmrich/PhotoEdit, (CR) Popperfoto/Alamy Images; **85** (TR) Hemera Technologies, (L) Stockdisc; **86** (B) ©Warren Bolster/Getty Images, (C) Blend Images/Getty Images, (CL) Katja Zimmermann/Getty Images, (CL) Ty Allison/Getty Images; **87** (TL) Dave Nagel/Getty Images; **88** Popperfoto/Alamy Images; **89** (TR) Bettmann/Corbis; **90** (BC) Bettmann/Corbis; **91** (BR) ©Hulton Archive/Getty Images, (TL) CORR/AFP/Getty Images, (BR) Fox Photos/Hulton Archive/Getty Images, (TR) Leonard de Salva/Corbis; **92** Bettmann/Corbis; **93** (T) Popperfoto/Alamy Images; **94** (B) AP/Wide World Photos; **95** (B) Bettman/Corbis, (TR) Hulton-Deutsch Collection/Corbis; **104** Bettmann/Corbis; **105** (T) Bob Daemmrich/PhotoEdit; **106** (B) Dimitri Iundt; TempSport/Corbis; **107** (T) Creasource/Corbis; **108** (R) Stockdisc; **109** The Granger Collection, NY; **110** (BR) Hulton-Deutsch Collection/Corbis, (CR) Johner/Getty Images, (TR) Stockdisc; **111** (BC) Jupiterimages/Thinkstock, (CL) White Cross Productions/Getty Images; **112** (B) Bettmann/Corbis, (T) Getty Images; **113** (TC) Corbis, (T) Getty Images, (BR) Philip Gould/Corbis; **114** (BL) Corbis, (T) Getty Images; **115** (T) AP/Wide World Photos; **116** (CL) Stockdisc; **117** (BR) ©Jeff Greenberg/Alamy Images, (CL) Bettmann/Corbis, (TL) Getty Images; **118** (BL) Bo Zaunders/Corbis, (TL) Johner/Getty Images; **119** (TR, B) Heidi Zeiger Photography; **120** (B) ©Chicago Daily News negatives collection, DN-0088479. Courtesy of the Chicago Historical Society/Library of Congress, (TR, T) Heidi Zeiger Photography; **121** (TR) DAJ/Getty Images, (BL) Heidi Zeiger Photography; **122** (C) ©Larry Dale Gordon/Getty Images, (TL, B) Heidi Zeiger Photography; **123** (TR) Hemera Technologies, (BR) Kay Berkson/©Changing Worlds; **132** (CR) ©Ariel Skelley/Corbis, (TL) ©David Samuel Robbins/Corbis, (BL) ©Royalty-Free/Corbis, (TL) Ashley Cooper/Corbis; **133** (TR) ©H. Armstrong Roberts/Corbis, (TL) Getty Images, (CL) Hulton-Deutsch Collection/Corbis; **134** (BC) White Cross Productions/Getty Images; **135** (B) Dimitri Iundt; TempSport/Corbis; **137** (CR) Geoff Brightling/DK Images; **138** (B) ©Larry Dale Gordon/Getty Images; **139** (CR) AP/Wide World Photos; **140** (CR) Harry Taylor/DK Images; **141** (T) Katja Zimmermann/Getty Images; **142** (CL) Steve Gorton/DK Images; **143** (C) Getty Images.

144